MW00898240

THIS NOTEBOOKS BELONGS TO:

Made in the USA
Middletown, DE
03 September 2020

18327965R00084